MAGICAL MYSTER
ABBEY ROAD • LET IT BE

MW00654424

Authentic new arrangements of songs from the albums

Arranged by TODD LOWRY

NEWLY RELEASED ON COMPACT DISC

This publication is not for sale in
the EC and/or Australia
or New Zealand.

HAL•LEONARD®
CORPORATION

7777 W. BLUEMOUND RD. P.O. BOX 13819 MILWAUKEE, WI 53213

Index of Songs
ALPHABETICALLY

MAGICAL MYSTERY TOUR
ABBEY ROAD • LET IT BE

Index of Songs
BY ALBUM

MAGICAL MYSTERY TOUR

Words and Music by
JOHN LENNON and PAUL McCARTNEY

With a beat

Roll up, roll up for the Magical Mystery Tour.
Step right this way.

Roll up,_____ Roll up__ for the mys-

- ter - y tour.___ Roll up,_____

THE FOOL ON THE HILL

Words and Music by
JOHN LENNON and PAUL McCARTNEY

FLYING

Words and Music by JOHN LENNON, PAUL McCARTNEY,
GEORGE HARRISON and RICHARD STARKEY

BLUE JAY WAY

Words and Music by
GEORGE HARRISON

I AM THE WALRUS

Words and Music by
JOHN LENNON and PAUL McCARTNEY

YOUR MOTHER SHOULD KNOW

Words and Music by
JOHN LENNON and PAUL McCARTNEY

HELLO, GOODBYE

Words and Music by
JOHN LENNON and PAUL McCARTNE

STRAWBERRY FIELDS FOREVER

Words and Music by
JOHN LENNON and PAUL McCARTNEY

Let me take you down____ 'cause I'm go-in' to____ Straw-ber-ry

Fields. Noth-ing is real, and noth-ing to get hung a-bout.

Straw-ber-ry Fields____ for-ev-er.____

PENNY LANE

Words and Music by JOHN LENNON
and PAUL McCARTNEY

38

40

BABY, YOU'RE A RICH MAN

Words and Music by
JOHN LENNON and PAUL McCARTNEY

ALL YOU NEED IS LOVE

Words and Music by
JOHN LENNON and PAUL McCARTNEY

There's noth-ing you can do that can't be done.___
There's noth-ing you can make that can't be made.___
There's noth-ing you can know that is-n't known.___

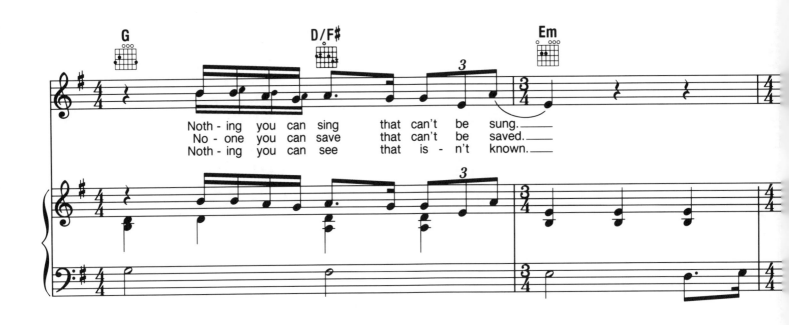

Noth-ing you can sing that can't be sung.___
No-one you can save that can't be saved.___
Noth-ing you can see that is-n't known.___

Noth-ing you can say but you can learn___ how to play the game___
Noth-ing you can do but you can learn___ how to be you in time
No-where you can be that is-n't where___ you're meant to be___

It's

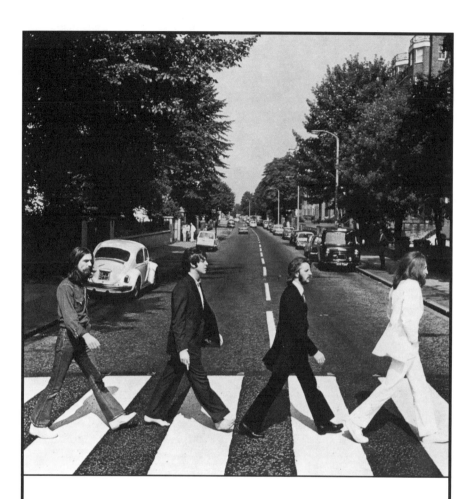

COME TOGETHER

Moderately slow, with a double-time feeling

Words and Music b
JOHN LENNON and PAUL McCARTNE

Here come old flat-top, He come groov-ing up slow-ly, He got Joo Joo eye-ball, He one

ho-ly roll-er, He got hair down to his knee.

Got to be a jok-er, He just do what he please.

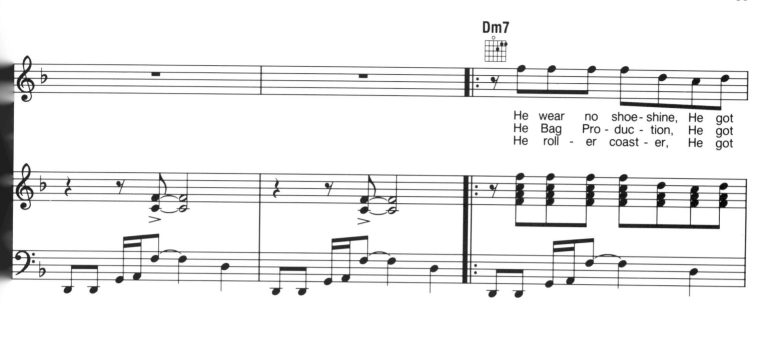

SOMETHING

Words and Music by
GEORGE HARRISON

Some- thing in____ the way____ she moves,____
Some- where in____ her smile____ she knows,____
Some- thing in____ the way____ she knows,____

at- tracts____ me like____ no oth- er lov - er.
that I____ don't need____ no oth- er lov - er.
and all____ I have____ to do is think____ of her.

Some- thing in____ the way____ she woos_____ me.____
Some- thing in____ her style____ that shows_____ me.
Some- thing in____ the things____ she shows_____ me.

I don't want to leave____ her now,

you

56

OH! DARLING

Words and Music by
JOHN LENNON and PAUL McCARTNEY

harm.

(Spoken) Believe me, darling

When you

I'll nev - er do you no harm.

MAXWELL'S SILVER HAMMER

Moderately (played as)

Words and Music by
JOHN LENNON and PAUL McCARTNEY

Joan was quiz-zi-cal, stud-ied pat-a-phys-i-cal
Back in school a-gain, Max-well plays the fool a-gain,
P. C. Thir-ty-one said, "We've caught a dir-ty one,"

sci- ence in the home___
teach- er gets an- noyed.___
Max- well stands a- lone___

Late nights all a- lone___
Wish- ing all to a- void___
Paint- ing tes- ti- mo-

___ with a test - tube, oh, oh, oh, oh.___
___ an un pleas- ant sce- e- e- ene,___
-ni- al pic - tures, oh, oh, oh, oh.___

Max - well Ed - i - son, ma - jor - ing in med - i - cine,
She tells Max to stay when the class has gone a - way.
Rose and Val - er - ie scream - ng from the gal - ler - y

calls her on the phone:___ "Can I take you out___
So he waits be - hind___ Writ - ing fif - ty times___
say he must go free.___ The judge does not a - gree___

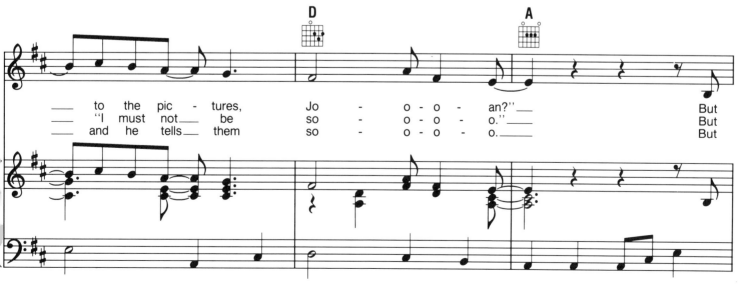

___ to the pic - tures, Jo - o - o - an?" ___ But
___ "I must not___ be so - o - o - o." ___ But
___ and he tells them so - o - o - o. ___ But

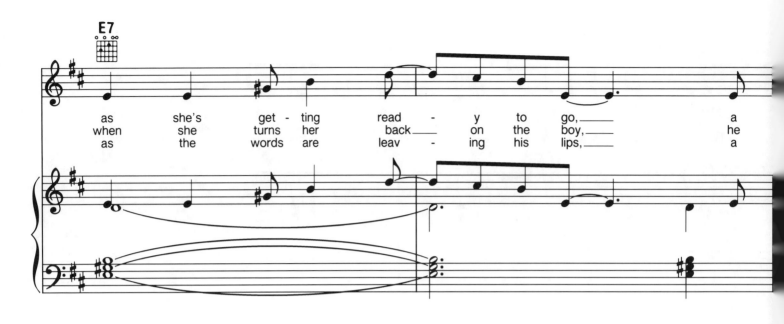

as she's get - ting read - y to go,____ a
when she turns her back____ on the boy,____ he
as the words are leav - ing his lips,____ a

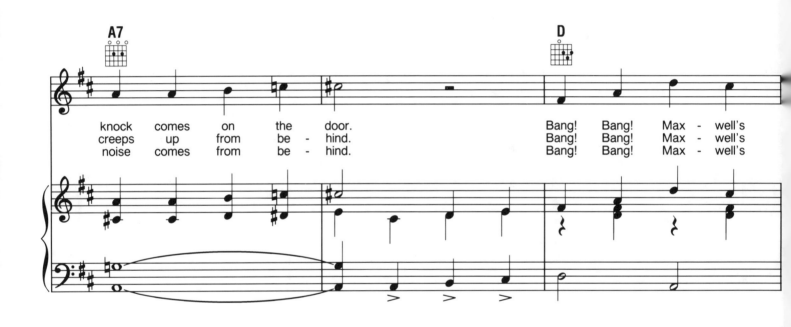

knock comes on the door. Bang! Bang! Max - well's
creeps up from be - hind. Bang! Bang! Max - well's
noise comes from be - hind. Bang! Bang! Max - well's

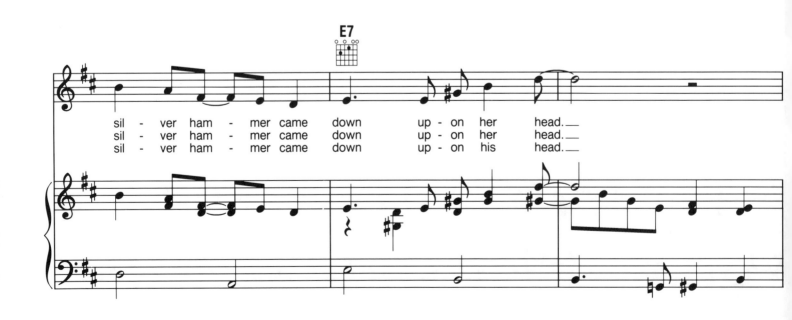

sil - ver ham - mer came down up - on her head.____
sil - ver ham - mer came down up - on her head.____
sil - ver ham - mer came down up - on his head.____

Sil - ver ham - mer.

OCTOPUS'S GARDEN

Moderately bright

Words and Music by
RICHARD STARKEY

I WANT YOU
(SHE'S SO HEAVY)

Words and Music by
JOHN LENNON and PAUL McCARTNEY

I want (1, 2, 4) you.

(3) (instrumental ad lib)

I want you so bad. I want

you. I want you so bad, it's

HERE COMES THE SUN

Words and Music by
GEORGE HARRISON

BECAUSE

Words and Music by
JOHN LENNON and PAUL McCARTNEY

Be - cause the world is round, it turns me
cause the wind is high, it blows my
cause the sky is blue, it makes me

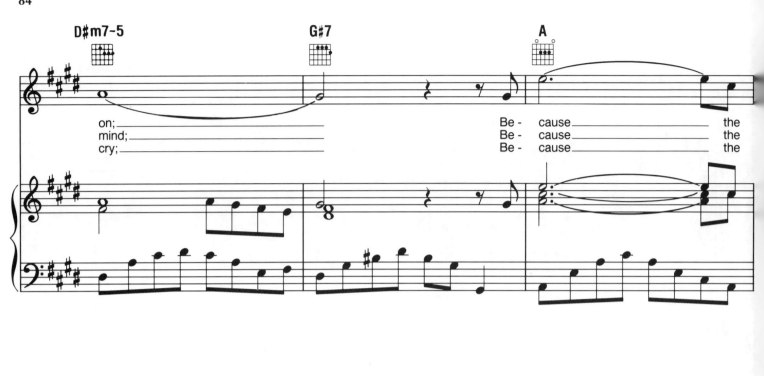

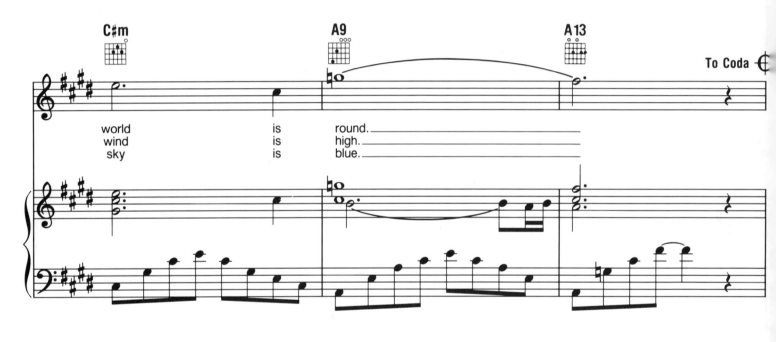

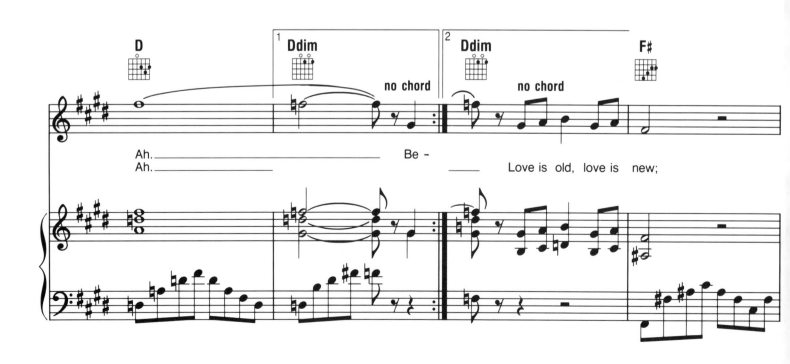

YOU NEVER GIVE ME YOUR MONEY

Words and Music by
JOHN LENNON and PAUL McCARTNEY

You nev-er give me your mon-ey,___
I nev-er give you my num-ber,___

You on-ly give me your fun-ny pa-per,
I on-ly give you my sit-u-a-tion,

And in the mid-dle of ne-
And in the mid-dle of in-

91

SUN KING

Words and Music by
JOHN LENNON and PAUL McCARTNEY

MEAN MR. MUSTARD

Words and Music by
JOHN LENNON and PAUL McCARTNEY

POLYTHENE PAM

Words and Music by
JOHN LENNON and PAUL McCARTNEY

Yeah,   yeah,   yeah.

SHE CAME IN THROUGH THE BATHROOM WINDOW

Words and Music by
JOHN LENNON and PAUL McCARTNEY

Moderately slow 4

She came in through the bath-room win-dow,___
And so I quit the p'lice de-part-ment,___

pro-tect-ed by a sil-ver spoon.___
and got my-self a stead-y job.___

But now she sucks her thumb and won-ders___ by the
And though she tried her best to help me.___ she could

GOLDEN SLUMBERS

Words and Music by
JOHN LENNON and PAUL McCARTNEY

THE END

Words and Music by JOHN LENNON
and PAUL McCARTNEY

Love you,— love you,—

109

110

HER MAJESTY

Words and Music by JOHN LENNON
and PAUL McCARTNEY

Her Maj - es - ty's a pret - ty nice girl, but she does - n't have a lot to say. ___ Her Maj - es - ty's a pret - ty nice girl, but she chang - es from day ___ to day. ___

CARRY THAT WEIGHT

Words and Music by
JOHN LENNON and PAUL McCARTNEY

LET IT BE

TWO OF US

Words and Music by
JOHN LENNON and PAUL McCARTNEY

122

the road_____ that stretch - es out_____ a - head.

(Spoken:) We're go-in' home.   Better believe it.   Goodbye.

Repeat and Fade

DIG A PONY

Words and Music by JOHN LENNON
and PAUL McCARTNEY

road hog.____
stone - y.____
lone - ly.____

Well you can pen - e - trate__ an - y place you
Well you can im - i - tate__ ev - 'ry-one you
Well you can syn - di - cate__ an - y boat you

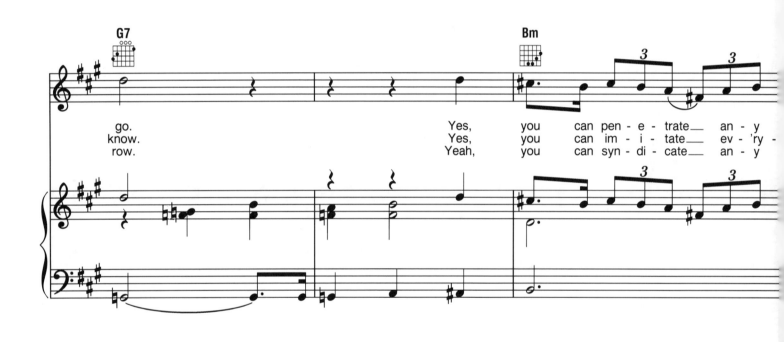

go.
know.
row.

Yes, you can pen - e - trate__ an - y
Yes, you can im - i - tate__ ev - 'ry -
Yeah, you can syn - di - cate__ an - y

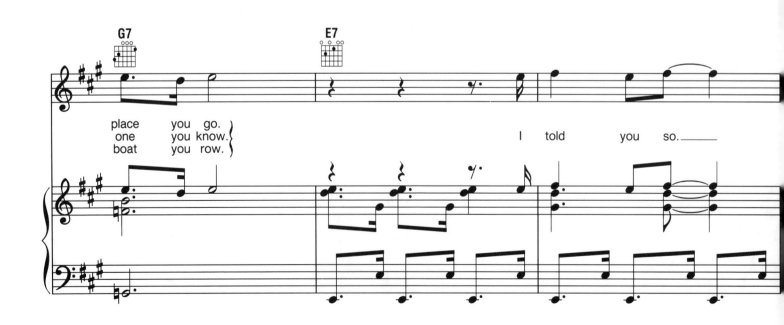

place you go. }
one you know. }
boat you row. }

I told you so.____

All   I   want   is   you,

Ev - 'ry-thing   has   got   to   be   just   like   you   want   it   to.

Slower
no chord   a tempo   To Coda

Be - cause

ACROSS THE UNIVERSE

Words and Music by
JOHN LENNON and PAUL McCARTNEY

133

I ME MINE

Words and Music by
GEORGE HARRISON

136

DIG IT

Words and Music by JOHN LENNON, PAUL McCARTNEY,
GEORGE HARRISON and RICHARD STARKEY

MAGGIE MAE

Arrangement by JOHN LENNON, PAUL McCARTNEY
GEORGE HARRISON and RICHARD STARKEY

LET IT BE

Words and Music by
JOHN LENNON and PAUL McCARTNEY

145

I'VE GOT A FEELING

Words and Music by JOHN LENNON
and PAUL McCARTNEY

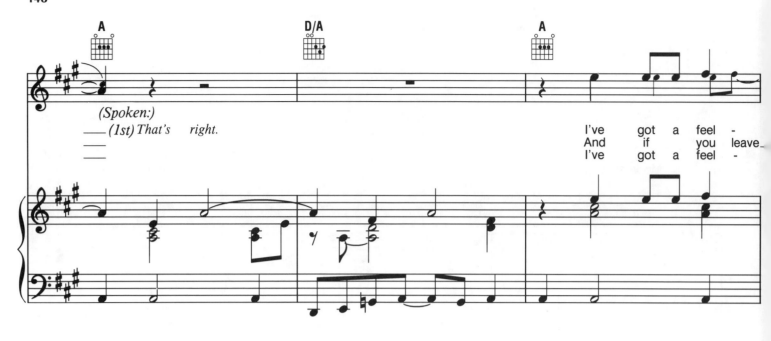

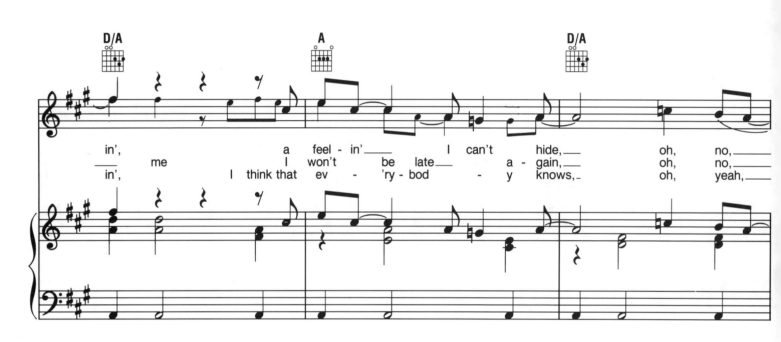

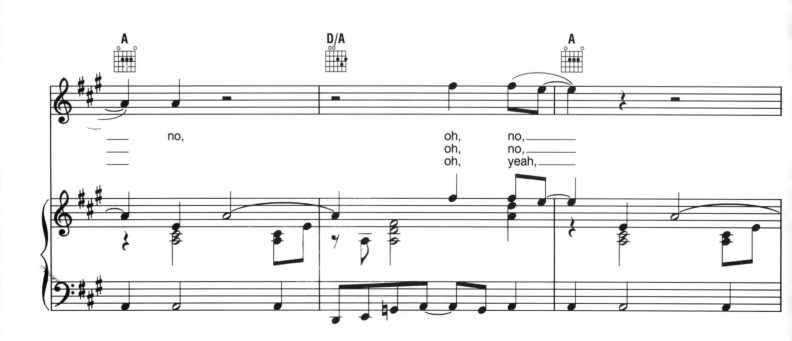

THE LONG AND WINDING ROAD

Words and Music by JOHN LENNON
and PAUL McCARTNEY

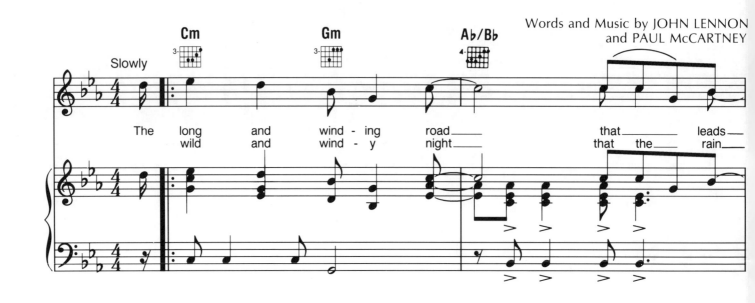

The long and wind-ing road____ that____ leads____
wild and wind-y night____ that the____ rain____

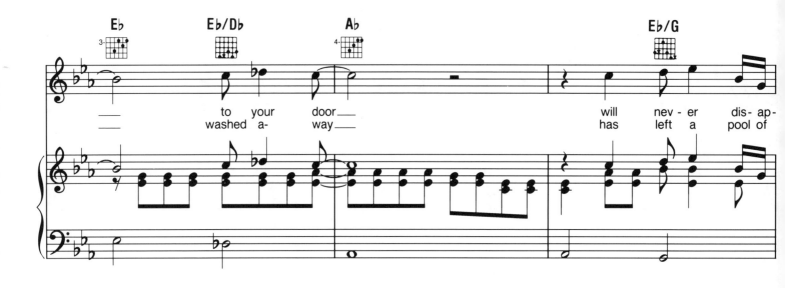

____ to your door____ will nev-er dis-ap-
____ washed a-way____ has left a pool of

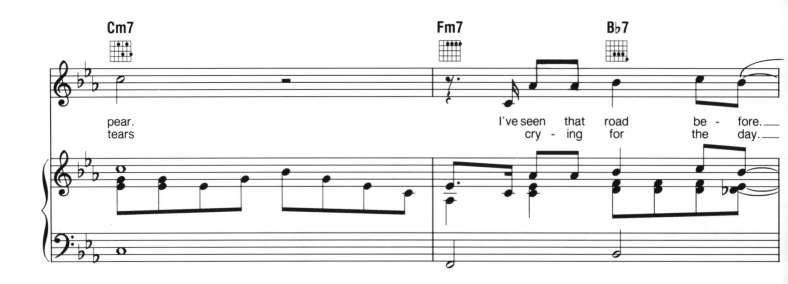

pear. I've seen that road be - fore.
tears cry - ing for the day.

FOR YOU BLUE

Words and Music by
GEORGE HARRISON

cause you're sweet_ and love - ly, girl, I love you._
want you in___ the morn - ing, girl, I love you._
loved you from___ the mo - ment_ I saw you._

(Spoken:) Elmore James got nothin' on this baby.

D.S. al Coda

CODA

Give it the blues.

GET BACK

Words and Music by
JOHN LENNON and PAUL McCARTNEY

ONE AFTER 909

Words and Music by
JOHN LENNON and PAUL McCARTNEY

1. My

1,4. ba - by said she's trav - 'llin' on the one af - ter Nine - O - Nine.
2. begged her not to go, and I begged her on my bend - ed knees.
3. she said she's trav - 'llin' on the one af - ter Nine - O - Nine.

I said, "Move o - ver, hon - ey, I'm
You're on - ly fool - in' round,
I said, a - "Move o - ver, hon - ey, I'm